Train Like a Ninja

Jon M. Fishman

Lerner Publications ◆ Minneapolis

Lerner Publications Company
An imprint of Lerner Publishing Group, Inc.
241 First Avenue North
Minneapolis, MN 55401 USA

For reading levels and more information, look up this title at www.lernerbooks.com.

Library of Congress Cataloging-in-Publication Data

Names: Fishman, Jon M., author.
Title: Train like a ninja / Jon M. Fishman.
Description: Minneapolis : Lerner Publications, [2020] | Series: Lightning bolt books — ninja mania | Includes bibliographical references and index. | Audience: Ages 6–9 | Audience: Grades 2–3 | Summary: "Ninja of the past learned to climb, dodge, and sneak. But how do modern ninja tackle intense obstacles? This title takes a fun look at ninja training, including martial arts techniques readers can try"— Provided by publisher.
Identifiers: LCCN 2019028772 (print) | LCCN 2019028773 (ebook) | ISBN 9781541577077 (library binding) | ISBN 9781541589193 (paperback) | ISBN 9781541583283 (ebook)
Subjects: LCSH: Martial arts—Training—Juvenile literature. | Hand-to-hand fighting, Oriental—Juvenile literature. | Ninja—Juvenile literature.
Classification: LCC GV1102.7.T7 F57 2020 (print) | LCC GV1102.7.T7 (ebook) | DDC 796.8071—dc23

LC record available at https://lccn.loc.gov/2019028772
LC ebook record available at https://lccn.loc.gov/2019028773

Manufactured in the United States of America
1-46729-47720-8/30/2019

Table of Contents

The Time of the Ninja

A ninja climbs a castle wall in the middle of the night. He reaches up and grabs the  edge of an open window with his fingertips. The ninja pulls himself into the castle.

Powerful families lived in palaces such as Hiroshima Castle.

Ninja were most active during the Sengoku, or Warring States, period in Japan. This was a time of war from the mid-fifteenth century to the seventeenth century. Important families in Japan fought to control the country.

Real ninja probably didn't wear clothing like this. They wore regular clothes to blend in.

Ninja worked for many different leaders during this time. Though they sometimes fought enemy soldiers, ninja most often acted as spies. They learned important secrets and destroyed supplies in enemy territory.

Ninja knew how to make medicine and weapons. They practiced sneaking into buildings and staying hidden.

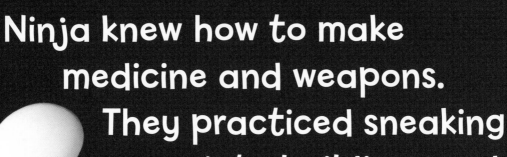

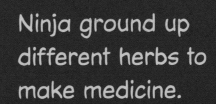

Ninja ground up different herbs to make medicine.

Ninja Stories

During the Sengoku period, ninja worked in secret. They dressed as farmers or laborers. They didn't want anyone to know they were ninja.

Myths about ninja arose in part because of their unusual skills.

Since ninja's lives were secret, people made up stories about them. The stories grew into myths. Some myths said ninja could disappear. Others said they could fly.

Ninja couldn't disappear, but they were trained to move quietly. They wore dark clothing at night to stay hidden.

Ninja did much of their work at night—but they spied during the day too.

Ninja also worked on their strength and balance.

Ninja couldn't fly, either. They practiced climbing walls and sneaking into buildings. Ninja were so good at climbing that it may have seemed as if they could fly!

Ninja in Action

A woman reaches to grab a platform above her. She pulls herself up as people cheer and clap with excitement. TV cameras catch every moment.

Modern ninja might train in gyms.

Some modern ninja are athletes. They compete in events around the world that people watch on TV. The athletes move and climb through obstacle courses like ninja of the past did.

With training, athletes can swing from obstacles without falling.

Many athletes train for these courses by rock climbing. They learn how to move while hanging above the ground. Rock climbing strengthens athletes' hands and arms.

Athletes practice many different obstacles in a gym. That way, they're ready for anything on an obstacle course.

Climbing skills are important to every kind of ninja!

Ninja Soldiers

Modern soldiers fight around the world in armies. Their training is like the ninja training of the past. Modern soldiers use ninja skills to help win wars.

Obstacle courses prepare soldiers to tackle real-life challenges.

Soldiers train on obstacle courses. They practice climbing over walls and jumping from one obstacle to another.

Soldiers learn to move quietly and carefully. They train to stay hidden in dangerous places. Camo clothing helps them stay out of sight.

Like ninja of the past, soldiers use their clothing to blend in.

Soldiers' training helps them hold on tight!

Soldiers have dangerous jobs. Ninja-like training helps them protect others and stay safe.

Real-Life Ninja

Ninja of the past didn't write down their methods. They passed on their knowledge by training new ninja.

When Jinichi Kawakami was six years old, a ninja master began training him. The ninja master taught him to walk quietly and sneak into buildings. Though he may be the last ninja, Kawakami has said he will not train anyone new.

Ninja Fun Facts

- People have hired spies for thousands of years. They even appear in ancient texts.

- In Japan, ninja were also called *shinobi*.

- Most ninja didn't use swords as they do in movies. They used any weapons they could find. At times, ninja even used guns and explosives.

Glossary

camo: colors made to disguise or hide

modern: from the present time

myth: a story about the past that may not be true

obstacle: an object that slows or stops progress

obstacle course: a path with a series of objects that slow or stop progress

rock climbing: climbing up a mountain or rocky cliff

supply: a tool, food, or other needed material

train: to practice skills to get better at them

Further Reading

Fishman, Jon M. *Real-Life Ninja*. Minneapolis: Lerner Publications, 2020.

Hansen, Grace. *Japan*. Minneapolis: Abdo Kids, 2019.

Japan
https://kids.nationalgeographic.com/explore/countries/japan/

Ninja Facts for Kids
https://kids.kiddle.co/Ninja

Ninja—Kids Web Japan
https://web-japan.org/kidsweb/explore/history/q4.html

Terp, Gail. *Ninja*. Mankato, MN: Black Rabbit Books, 2020.

Index

Photo Acknowledgments

Image credits: davidf/Getty Images, p. 2; BLOOM image/Getty Images, p. 4; Christian Kober/ John Warburton-Lee Photography Ltd/Getty Images, p. 5; Drazen_/Getty Images, p. 6; Science Photo Library/Getty Images, p. 7; Christoph Hetzmannseder/Getty Images, p. 8; lisegagne/Getty Images, p. 9; PamelaJoeMcFarlane/Getty Images, p. 10; John S Lander/ LightRocket/Getty Images, p. 11; Tommaso Boddi/WireImage/Getty Images, p. 12; US Air Force photo/Samuel King Jr, p. 13; SolStock/Getty Images, p. 14; Lewis Geyer/Digital First Media/Boulder Daily Camera/Getty Images, p. 15; US Air Force photo/Senior Airman Joseph Pick, p. 16; US Air Force photo/Senior Airman Brian J. Ellis, p. 17; U.S. Army photo by Pfc. Jorge Reyes, p. 18; Airubon/Getty Images, p. 19; Kazuhiro Nogi/AFP/Getty Images, p. 20; metamorworks/Getty Images, p. 22.

Cover: Mostovyi Sergii Igorevich/Shutterstock.com.

Main body text set in Billy Infant regular. Typeface provided by SparkType.